Christmas is giving,
gifts under the tree
and time spent together,
just you and me.

Christmas is joy
that's overflowing.

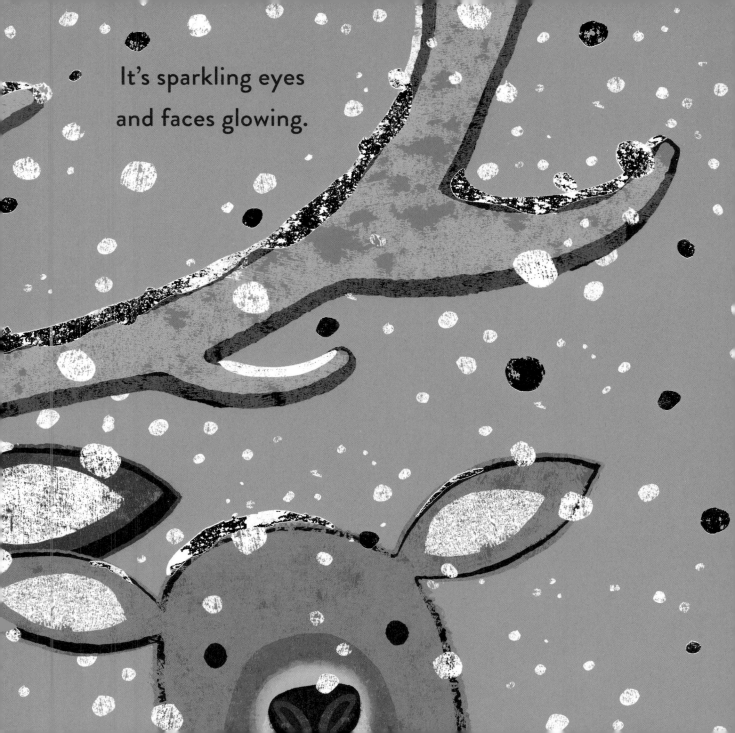

It's sparkling eyes
and faces glowing.

Christmas is sharing

laughter and fun

and being with family,
old and young.

Christmas is happiness,
smiles of surprise . . .

. . . the warm, loving glow
that lights up your eyes.

Christmas is kisses
and snuggles so tight;
the wonderful feeling
that everything's right.

Christmas is love
that lasts all year.

It's all of us,
together, here.

Christmas is peace,
stars twinkling above . . .